W9-BWP-090

MORE LETTERS FOR EVERY OCCASION

MORE LETTERS FOR EVERY OCCASION

—

A PASTOR'S SOURCEBOOK

—

JAMES E. TAYLOR III

Abingdon Press
Nashville

MORE LETTERS FOR EVERY OCCASION
A PASTOR'S SOURCEBOOK

Copyright © 2011 by Abingdon Press

All rights reserved.
No part of this work may be reproduced or transmitted in any form or by any means, electronic or mechanical, including photocopying and recording, or by any information storage or retrieval system, except as may be expressly permitted by the 1976 Copyright Act or in writing from the publisher. Requests for permission should be addressed to Abingdon Press, P.O. Box 801, 201 Eighth Avenue South, Nashville, TN 37202-0801 or permissions@umpublishing.org.

This book is printed on acid-free paper.

Library of Congress Cataloging-in-Publication Data

Taylor, James E., III
    More letters for every occasion : a pastor's sourcebook / James E. Taylor, III.
        p.   cm.
    ISBN 978-1-4267-1007-0 (pbk. : alk. paper)
1. Church correspondence.   2. Clergy—Correspondence.   3. Form letters.   I. Title.
    BV652.9.T39 2011
    253′.7—dc22

                                                                        2010047459

11 12 13 14 15 16 17 18 19 20—10 9 8 7 6 5 4 3 2 1
MANUFACTURED IN THE UNITED STATES OF AMERICA

Contents

IV. LETTERS RELATING TO PASTORAL CARE

V. LETTERS RELATING TO STEWARDSHIP AND FINANCE

VI. LETTERS RELATING TO ADMINISTRATION

VII. LETTERS RELATING TO COMMUNITY OUTREACH

VIII. ELECTRONIC COMMUNICATION

Acknowledgments

If you are listed below, you deserve your own letter from me as a way to express my sincere thanks for your investment in me as a person, pastor, and friend. Until those letters come, please know how pleased I am to have you in my life.

To my friends: Jesse, Marc, Chris, Aaron, Brenna, Quin, and Joe—thanks for putting up with me. Also, big thanks to the Aprentis Crew: Pat, CJ, Ben, Matt, Andrew, Deidre, and Lyle.

To my professors: James Bryan Smith, Anathea Portier-Young, Laceye Warner, and Joe Bessler. I hope you know how grateful I am.

To the Kansas West Conference: Gary Brooks, Cheryl Bell, Dianne Tombaugh, Craig Hauschild, Rick Just, Kevin Hopkins, Andrew Conard, David Smith, and Bishop Jones. You have blessed me in ways that can never be returned.

To my family: Jeff, Terry, Anthony, Melissa, and Mom—I love you guys! Dan and Sarah, Justin and Krysha, Katie and Tyler—thanks for letting me be a part of something so fun. Jeff and Theresa, Vicki and Robert, Mike and Sandra, thanks for being there for "Little" Jeff and Jimmy.

Edyn, you are certainly an "Echo of Eden." And Kassi—being a husband to you and a dad to Edyn is the greatest gift I've ever received. (If anyone is reading this and wondering why I didn't say to my wife and baby, "You're the greatest gift next to Jesus," know that Jesus doesn't need the publicity. Jesus knows he is my hero.)

Thanks to Charles Kyker, Bill Quick, and Adam Hamilton for offering your encouragement.

Last, to Skip and Kathy Armistead: Skip, thanks for the letters. Kathy, thanks for going above and beyond.

Introduction

Dear Reader,

At my house is a safe my brother bought me for Christmas. I never wrote a letter to my brother thanking him for the gift. So, Jeff, in the event that a forest fire or meteor hits my house, my safe is safe. Thanks.

If you are reading this, you may be asking yourself, what does he have that is so important that he needs a safe? Jewels? Money? None of the above. I spent all my money on the real jewels of my life, my wife and daughter, Kassi and Edyn. What sits in my safe are photos, cards, and letters my Dad gave to me. He died a few years back, and the letters he sent me remain the greatest trophies I have. I also keep cards and letters I've received from other people. Whereas I will delete emails, I will never toss out a letter.

If you doubt the sheer importance of letters, think about how vacuous our Scriptures would be had someone tossed out letters sent from Paul. I will go on record today in saying there were probably many more letters that might have been included in the canon had someone not thrown them away. Or used them for a second-century coffee coaster.

Take some time to think about just how meaningful letters really are. At the conclusion of this book, I think you'll be sold on letter writing.

The book you hold in your hands contains within it dozens of letters meant to aid you in your letter-writing endeavors. Two of the greatest complaints parishioners have regarding their service in the church is that (1) they don't sense adequate communication and (2) they don't receive any approbation or thanks from anyone. These letters will help you respond to the heartfelt needs of your parishioners and close friends.

I have heard it said that ninety percent of communication is miscommunication. Meaning, only ten percent of what we are trying to communicate is actually received. The letters within this book have been carefully crafted to help combat the communication barriers that so often stifle us. There are times when great pastoral concern should be communicated, and there are times when great leadership and visioning need to be communicated. And while pastors and lay leaders should do as much face-to-face communicating as possible, letters will help inform people while they are away from you.

Use these letters when you are stressed and need a guide. Use these letters for new ministry ideas. Use these letters to help you deal with tense situations. Use these letters to spur on more letter writing.

May the content of these letters assist you as you go forward to bless others with your time and with your words.

Be Blessed,

Jim

For online access, use this URL:
www.AbingdonPress.com/Taylor.Letters.PDF

I. Letters Relating to Church Leadership

Dear Christian Friends,

Part of my job as pastor is to help us all grow in our Christian faith. For me it's all about making disciples of Jesus Christ to transform the world. As you know, that is how we open each worship service, and that is how I want to be remembered after I leave here. I want people to say, "That Pastor Jim, he was all about helping people live the abundant life that Jesus talked about." Perhaps you'd like to be remembered that way too, so here is my vision about how, together, we can continue to move in that direction.

One thing I know that none of us want. None of us wants to be mediocre. We don't like sports teams that win just half their games. We don't want the best and brightest among us to be satisfied with only making Cs in school. And we don't want to stand before our Maker and say that we were satisfied to act like a Christian half the time.

When we go to God to ask for help, hope, and healing, we want to know we can count on God's all-sufficient and completely amazing grace. I believe God wants us to do our best to the best of our ability.

God has blessed this congregation with many gifts. I can't help but think about our dedicated staff of volunteers. Do you know that this week members of our church made fifteen hospital calls, delivered 100 meals, tutored thirty children in our after-school program, and attended the United Methodist Women's school for mission? The men of our church built a wheelchair ramp; our youth cut grass and weeded a neighbor's yard. Our church sent $500 to our Conference for missions across the world for places such as Haiti and Africa University.

We helped four families with utilities and delivered fifty pounds of food to the local food bank. And these are just the things I know about that we regularly do. I'm sure many of you are in mission where you are at work, home, or school.

Changing people's lives is what Jesus meant by offering salvation and sharing the good news of his love and mercy. So it worries me when we spend our time obsessing over things that are not worth considering. And it concerns me that sometimes we are too easily satisfied being so-so in our faith. I don't know about you, but I do not want us to be known for offering God's *somewhat* amazing grace.

From this day forward, I am dedicated to turning up the joy and enthusiasm around here. I encourage you to do the same. Actually, some of that is beginning to happen. Because of your dedication to shine the light of Christ in this community, the church leadership team has decided to go back to the drawing board to reimagine next year's programs. It is becoming clear that all of us want our light to shine. We want to be a church that helps seekers grow to be fully devoted followers and servants of Christ.

Everything that I do as a pastor, from checking my email, to preparing for sermons, to praying for you, will occur to help us fulfill that vision. And every event that we plan will be fueled by the passion to reach seekers and help them grow as disciples. If you have questions about the vision, please let me know. If you would like to give input to our leadership team, please contact me. We strive to bring God great delight. After all, we offer ministry in God's name and we want to be faithful followers.

My hope is that God's grace will continue to propel us into the future God has for us so that we will help seekers grow to be fully devoted followers and servants of Christ.

Too Excited!
Pastor Jim

CHRIST CHURCH

2010 RURAL HILL ROAD
STANDING STONE, MISSISSIPPI 37067
258.555.7664
WWW.CHRISTCHURCHMS.ORG

Dear Fellow Disciples,

This particular piece of Christ's body has been busy making giant waves for the kingdom of God! We are on our way—embarked on a journey. Today we are closer to fulfilling our God-given vision to turn seekers into fully devoted followers and servants of Christ.

Let me bring you up-to-date about what is happening:

• On August 23, we hosted a block party. More than seventy unchurched friends came out for that event! Seeds were planted.

• Then over Labor Day weekend, we hosted a Christian concert attended by over 40 unchurched seekers.

• Upcoming events include: a float in the Veterans' Parade, a Christmas concert, a SuperBowl Party, a Science Show, monthly community meals (free, of course), coffee chats, and a special sermon series on the theology of rock songs (yes, really). On top of these incredibly exciting and fun events for our unchurched neighbors, we will increase our small-group ministry to include divorce recovery and widows/widowers groups. In addition, we will offer an Alpha course and another DISCIPLE Bible Study.

A year ago we cast a vision that would help us increase our efforts in the areas of evangelism and discipleship. Today we celebrate that we are a step closer to that goal. But we are not even close to being done. Don't hang up your spurs yet. Things are just getting cranked up around here.

Save these dates: January 5-6. Please plan to come out to the church retreat on January 5-6. Leave your calendars and cell phones at home. We'll be dreaming big goals. We'll get to the calendars later!

If you have a life-changing story regarding the ways in which you've seen this church bless your life, your family, or your friends, let me know. We glorify the kingdom by recognizing ways in which God is at reign and at work. Often the best way to reach me is by emailing me at pastorjim@church.org.

Blessed to Be a Blessing,

Pastor Jim

9005 West Park Avenue
Poughkeepsie, NY 00225-5674
364-573-9473
WWW.TRINITYCHURCHNY.ORG

Dear Church Family,

During this past year our church made significant steps toward fulfilling our mission to make disciples for Jesus Christ to transform the world. Here is my year-end report giving some of the highlights.

Of the many things I did this year, speaking with the children at Vacation Bible School about Christ coming into their lives was the most moving. Speaking of VBS, this past year we tripled attendance of students and doubled our teacher participation! Thank you to the staff of fifty volunteers that made our VBS so successful.

Over the past year I counseled and married two couples. I presided over seven funerals, including the funeral of an eight-month-old baby. Many of you know this family and we all are still grieving the loss. I made countless hospital visits and spent many hours in prayer.

Forty-seven sermons were prepared and delivered. The most commented-on sermon was a play on the old question, "What's on Your Tombstone?"

Attendance has not radically increased, but we have added three new families to the church roll; and the people who are present have experienced the fullness of God in our midst. Financial giving has increased thanks to our lay-led stewardship program; small-group involvement is up. We have added a divorce recovery small group. I led the annual summer mission trip, assisted with a variety of youth functions, and also made dozens of home visits and phone calls.

In addition, I have been active on the Conference Committee on Evangelism, Board of Ordained Ministry, and on our town's ministerial association.

I have read thirty books and participated in our Conference Pastor's School as part of my continuing education.

Like many of the laity of our church, I have worked to bring new people to Christ, putting in about sixty hours a week.

All in all, it has been a busy, but fruitful year.

In the next year, I plan to focus on making more contacts with people outside of our church walls. My goal is to welcome two new members to our church every month. I also plan on creating better ways the entire church can participate in visitation and pastoral care.

Worship and preaching will continue getting stronger as I utilize multisensory resources. I promise to continue working on my leadership and communication skills while delegating appropriately those things that diminish my effectiveness as a minister to this church.

Just Getting Started,
Pastor Jim

Calvary Church of Christ

ONE WINDSOR COMMONS
GREEN HILLS, KENTUCKY 54399
364-573-9473
WWW.CALVARYCHURCHOFCHRIST.ORG

Dear Christian Friends,

Some people have fallen into the habit of believing Jesus to be a man who lived in deep poverty without resources. And while Jesus was continually on the road, without a place to lay his head, Jesus had money. He had enough money to utilize a full-time treasurer, a treasurer who happened to be stealing from him.

Our God is not short of cash. Let's stop living as if the kingdom needs a capital campaign to bail it out. Some churches may need that. But the kingdom of God has never been in the red. The kingdom of God is in the black every year, gaining momentum and interest.

Instead of sharing week-to-week bad news about the budget deficit in the bulletin, let's start sharing ways in which God is changing people's lives. Instead of mentioning the budget problems every single week, let's try getting our people excited about giving to the church.

People want to give; they just want to give to places that are going to use their money well. People want to give to places that are changing lives of children and youth. People want to give to a church that loves God more than it loves its steeples, carpets, and pews. Those things are important. But no one wants to give to a church so that it can buy new banners. People want to give with the hope that God will use the money to increase the population of heaven.

So this week, instead of focusing on what we don't have, let's focus on the blessings God is giving us and on the coming of God's kingdom.

Let's get to it!

Pastor Jim

FAITH BRETHREN CHURCH

776 WILLOWBROOK LANE, CUMBERLAND, ILLINOIS / 364-573-9473 / WWW.FAITHBRETHRENCHURCH.ORG

Dear Visiting Leader,

I know that your schedule makes it difficult to do all the things you want to do, let alone all the things that others ask of you. With that in mind, I just want to communicate my utmost appreciation for your upcoming visit. It will do a lot to invigorate our congregation.

Just to be clear, we are expecting your arrival on Sunday, March 1, at 10:45 A.M. We've reserved a parking place for you. It is clearly marked, and I'll be on hand to greet you with a good cup of coffee in hand. For your convenience, I'm enclosing directions to the church. Just a reminder, though, there is a lot of road construction on I-40.

Also in honor of your time with us, we plan to submit a donation to the local food pantry in your name.

Please let me know if you have any materials you'd like us to hand out. We should have adequate time for a brief run-through before the service starts. If there are any questions or changes, please let me know.

Again, we are looking forward to seeing you soon.

May Christ's Arms Enfold You with Love,
Jim

ST. JOHN'S
COMMUNITY CHURCH

5008 ROSA PARKS BOULEVARD, NASHVILLE, TENNESSEE

615-555-9473 / WWW.STJOHNSNASHVILLE.ORG

Dear Church Member,

There seems to be a rumor going around that summer is a time for the church to shut down, kick back, relax, and wait until after Labor Day to get going again. While some of us do plan to go on vacation, if anything, the summer also gives families more time for family activities at the church.

Here at St. John's Community Church, we do not take our summer off. In fact, we crank up our opportunities.

- This year we are planning to do two Vacation Bible Schools, with the hope of attracting different groups of kids. If children plan to repeat, that will just give us a chance to help them take these incredible songs and teachings even deeper.

- We will offer a one-day family retreat during the month of June. Details will be in the Sunday morning bulletin and bi-weekly newsletter.

- For those of you who can't get enough Bible study, we plan to offer a DISCIPLE Bible Study on Thursday nights at 7:00.

- There will also be a study for youth and children on Wednesday nights.

- The youth will go on a mission project. This year they are going to Mountain Top.

- We plan a family trip to an amusement park on July 10. Details will be forthcoming soon.

- We will host a weekly community game night at the church. Please plan to bring your board games. They will be on Wednesday nights, beginning on June 5. We plan to put some information in the newspaper about this as well.

If, however, you plan to vacation at your lake or beach house, you can do a couple things: (1) be actively involved in a church where you are and (2) invite your incredibly innovating and loving pastor for a visit!

If you have other program ideas, please come to the Summer Extravaganza planning meeting that is taking place next Wednesday night, May 2. Also feel free to submit ideas at the church website, www.stjohnsnashville.org, or email me at pastorjim@church.org.

Thanks so much.

Looking forward to all the summer fun!

Pastor Jim

CENTRAL
BAPTIST
CHURCH

201 WEST MAIN ST., HENDERSON, NEVADA 89015
(702) 555-1200 / WWW.CENTRALBAPTISTCHURCHNV.ORG

Dear Friends and Members of Central Baptist Church,

As we approach the season of Advent, I want to offer a word of explanation so that our celebration will be more meaningful this year. It is my hope that a fuller understanding of Advent will bring you closer to God and help you experience the Holy Spirit in a powerful way.

The season of Advent has a long and honorable history in the Christian faith. Over the centuries, its celebration has touched millions of people. Today Advent is celebrated as a season of expectant and joyful longing for the fulfillment of God's promised reign, as we wait for the One who has already come. The word *advent* means "arrival that has been awaited" (especially of something momentous). For us in the church, Advent is the four Sundays that precede Christmas. It is meant to be something unbridled, something exciting, even adventurous.

Chances are when your parents knew you were on the way, they immediately began preparing a way for your coming. They may have decorated a nursery, painted walls, purchased a crib. And they waited and counted down the days until finally—a glorious day!

In Advent we prepare the way of the Lord. We renovate our souls so that our hearts may prepare him room. And finally, a glorious dawn breaks, shattering the darkness. God comes near; Emmanuel, "God is with us." This is Advent. And it is anything but dull. Make this Advent what it is meant to be, an adventure!

So get to renovating your heart. Recover that old couch, clean up the yard, sweep off the porch, set the table for a banquet. Christ is coming!

Alleluia,

Pastor Jim

EMMANUEL LUTHERAN CHURCH

107 BUBBLING BROOK DRIVE
BREEZEVILLE CITY, TEXAS 77443
173-555-4323 / WWW.EMMANUELLUTHERANTX.ORG

Dear Member,

This Lent, your devotional life is going to change. Which means your day-to-day routine should also be warned: a change is on the horizon.

Here is some background about Lent and why we celebrate it. The church in Rome and North Africa had three weeks of preparation before Easter for those being baptized. Other parts of the early church also held three-week baptismal preparations at various times of the year. At the Council of Nicaea in 325 A.D., these fasts were combined into what we know as the season of Lent. Throughout history, Lent has varied in length, but it lasts about forty days and it was meant as a time of fasting. However, Sundays were still little Easters and, hence, not part of the Lenten fast. Traditional Lenten practices include the use of purple vestments and kneeling for prayers (both symbolizing penitence), and the omissions of certain words, for example, "Alleluia." For us, Lenten disciplines might include cutting back on watching TV or not playing computer games.

Historically, Fat Tuesday, the day before Lent begins, meant going out and indulging in pleasure.

This year I invite you to consider a form of fasting and repentance for Lent. Pick something in your life that you know needs to go. Don't pick something easy like chocolate or soda pop. Go without gossip or sarcasm or judgment or anger. And then take it a step further and go without those things that are just terrible for your physical body.

Then, if you are able, join me and let's take it a step farther. On top of going without something for forty days, I also want you to make a spiritual *addition* to your devotional life— preferably something that might parallel what you are going without. If you plan to go forty days without TV, which would be great considering the average American spends 28 hours per week watching TV, plan on reading ten books of the Bible. If you plan on going without pizza, pop, or chocolate, plan on exercising forty minutes a day. Or if a parallel is not there, just plan on adding something—pray for your annoying coworker, pray for a politician you dislike, do a good deed in secret, give away some of your valued possessions.

Your life is about to change. And in forty days, with God's help, you will be the person you've always wanted to be, living the life you've always wanted.

Your Fellow Servant in Christ,

Pastor Jim

II. Letters Relating to Preaching and Worship

Dear Ben,

I want, first of all, to thank you for your passion for God. Seeing your commitment reminds me I am not alone in mine.

Second, I thank you for listening so closely to the sermon I preached recently. Sometimes I wonder if anyone is listening at all. The fact that you found something to disagree with is a reminder to me of the awesome task of preaching. And it is a reminder that, yes, people are listening.

I want you to know that I take your concern very seriously and would like to talk further about it. Are you available any time this week for a cup of coffee? I'd love to hear more about your understanding of this scripture. I'm always open to learning more from other people's experience.

For any distress I caused you, I ask your forgiveness. Please remember that you and I are both on a journey.

In the spirit of mutual love and accountability, let's get together soon for fellowship and conversation. How about Thursday, 2:15 P.M. at Pete's restaurant?

Looking forward to it!

Bring your hermeneutical boxing gloves! (Kidding.) This is going to be great.

Yours in Christ,
Pastor Jim

CHRIST CHURCH

2010 RURAL HILL ROAD
STANDING STONE, MISSISSIPPI 37067
258.555.7664
WWW.CHRISTCHURCHMS.ORG

Dear Friend,

I want to thank you for taking the time to raise a concern regarding the volume of the music. As pastor, I am usually located closer to the front than the back, so I never know if the volume is too loud or too soft. I depend on people like you to let us know how we are doing.

Your complaint is that the guitar and drums are too loud. This is such a difficult problem. While I admit that sometimes the volume does get a tad loud for my tastes, I come back to the fact that we are doing our best in order to reach as many new people as possible. I suspect that you know that our church has as part of its mission to reach new seekers so that we will become faithful followers of Jesus. To reach them, we have to be willing to compromise some of our preferences. But at the same time, we have a responsibility to care for our existing congregation. We certainly don't want to alienate people.

To help us address this issue, would you be interested in serving on a committee to look at the entire service? Your love for this church and passion to see that we get things right make you a perfect person for this.

Please consider it. And please join me in helping solve this dilemma.

Yours in Christ,
Pastor Jim

Trinity Church

9005 WEST PARK AVENUE
POUGHKEEPSIE, NY 00225-5674
364-573-9473
WWW.TRINITYCHURCHNY.ORG

Dear Fellow Worshipers,

We are a warm and friendly church and, in the coming weeks, we are going to have ample opportunities to demonstrate the love of Christ. I want to invite you to participate in extending hospitality to our newly invited guests so that they will feel not only welcome but also accepted and nourished. We want them to leave the church feeling like they met God face-to-face. But this takes a lot of preparation. We must prepare our own hearts and minds, so I am writing you to ask that in the coming two weeks you will join me and pray, daily, that our guests will find God in a powerful way in our midst.

Beginning next Sunday we expect guests to visit our morning worship service. I'm sure you agree that we want these people to experience the love of Christ the moment they step out of their cars in the parking lot. They do not care how much we know until they know that we care.

On my end, I'll make sure the sermons are the best possible. (God help us!) We have special music planned, and the worship committee is busy finishing the new altar cloths. Thanks to the trustees, the parking lot has new signs for visitor parking, and we have a team of people who have agreed to be parking lot attendants. In addition, several of you have already agreed to greet people as they enter and direct them to a Sunday school class or to the sanctuary.

As you can see, there is already a lot under way. For your part, I ask that you and your family plan to be present at worship for the next four weeks, because a full sanctuary communicates that we are serious about our commitment to the Lord. And naturally, we will have refreshments in the Fellowship Hall between Sunday school and worship. For the next month, all refreshments will be free thanks to an anonymous donor.

Get pumped! Lives are about to change. And our church has something to do with that!

If you want to help or can think of anything else we need to do, please attend the Radical Hospitality meeting, Wednesday night at 7:00, here in my office. Or email me at pastorjim@church.org.

Hope to see you there,
Pastor Jim

Calvary Church of Christ

ONE WINDSOR COMMONS
GREEN HILLS, KENTUCKY 54399
364-573-9473
WWW.CALVARYCHURCHOFCHRIST.ORG

Dear Teacher,

You do a lot for our children and our community. So we would like to invite you to a special worship service on Sunday, October 12, at 11:00 A.M. at Calvary Church of Christ. I've enclosed directions for your convenience. At this service, we plan to honor teachers in our school district. This is one way that we can say thank you for all that you do in educating our children.

During the service, a number of students will briefly talk about what their favorite teacher means to them. After the service, we will have a covered-dish dinner; although it probably doesn't beat the cafeteria food or delicious delights found in the teacher's lounge, if my wife is to be believed, but it will have to do!

Please let me know whether you and your family might be able to attend this special service!

Sincerely,
Pastor Jim

ALDERSGATE
UNITED METHODIST CHURCH

23 WEST CRESCENT BOULEVARD, DENTON, OH 77443
173-555-4323 / WWW.ALDERSGATEUMCHURCH.ORG

Dear Sheila,

Thank you for agreeing to serve on this year's worship committee. It is my hope that, with your help, we will make our services more exciting. So before we meet, please take a few minutes to think about these things:

- What would make people want to get out of bed every Sunday and come to worship?
- How can we make our services incredibly innovative?
- How can we help our congregation experience the grace and goodness of God every Sunday?
- What is the heartfelt need of every individual in our congregation?
- What are they dying to hear?
- How can we fashion our service in such a way that it becomes the greatest single hour of a person's week?
- How does God speak to you through worship?

Please pray about these questions for the next two weeks.

As we do this, and as we continually evaluate and sharpen our efforts, the quality of our Sunday morning adventure will increase. God will be pleased with that—after all, God deserves our best. Our goal is to help people experience the presence of the living God in fresh and powerful ways.

I'll bring my answers to these questions as well. I'm looking forward to working with you on this important matter.

May God Bless and Keep You,
Pastor Jim

FAITH BRETHREN CHURCH

776 WILLOWBROOK LANE, CUMBERLAND, ILLINOIS / 364-573-9473 / WWW.FAITHBRETHRENCHURCH.ORG

Dear Child,

On this day, November 23, 2012, you were baptized into a community of believers called Christians at Faith Brethren Church. This practice is a long tradition of the church—over two thousand years old. That is a long time!

Your parents love you so much. And I want you to know that God loves you too!

There were dozens of people present at your baptism—some young, some old—but all children of God. So, guess what? Because they are all children of God, they are your brothers and sisters in this great faith! And these are people you can call upon as you mature in faith. They will care for you if you ever need their help.

Until that day know that your parents are the people God brought into your life to help you grow strong. Listen to them; respect them.

I can't wait to see the ministry God calls you to as you grow up. Maybe you'll be a teacher, a pastor, an artist, or something else. In any case, it all started with your baptism today.

May God surround you with a loving family and friends, and may you embrace the future God has for you.

Sincerely,
Pastor Jim

Dear Michelle,

Your baptism marks a great day for St. John's Community Church. The act of baptism stands out in my mind as the greatest of all Christian celebrations and victories. It may have been a while ago, maybe even years, that you said yes to God. But at your baptism, the congregation was able to physically see what you have experienced inwardly, God's love and forgiveness.

Thank you for saying yes to God. Your life has always been in the hands of God, but now you are responding with a commitment to be a disciple of Jesus Christ. As you go about doing your job, typing on the computer, changing diapers, giving pats on the back and handshakes, being with family and friends, you do so participating with Christ in the ministry of reconciliation. You are now charged with the task of handing food to the hungry and water to the thirsty. You have been called upon to serve in the Royal Priesthood. Some say you've been called out of darkness to serve in the light. I agree with that. Shine like the brightest star in the heavens.

May the glory of your resurrected life burn brightly as you now help guide others to God's unfailing love.

Much Love This Day,
Pastor Jim

III. Letters Relating to Membership and Visitors

CENTRAL BAPTIST CHURCH

201 WEST MAIN ST., HENDERSON, NEVADA 89015
(702) 555-1200 / WWW.CENTRALBAPTISTCHURCHNV.ORG

Dear New Church,

It is with great sadness that we release _____ from our records as a member of Central Baptist Church. We are sad to see her go. But her gifts and graces will make her an invaluable part of your faith community. We wish her the best. And we wish your church continued success with its mission and ministry to bring Christ's peace, love, and justice to our world.

Thanks so much,
Pastor Jim

EMMANUEL
LUTHERAN
CHURCH

107 BUBBLING BROOK DRIVE
BREEZEVILLE CITY, TEXAS 77443
173-555-4323 / WWW.EMMANUELLUTHERANTX.ORG

Dear Mr. Sanchez,

I am thrilled to let you know what is happening at our church. Recently five young children were baptized into the faith, our youth group went on a mission trip to Chicago, the church website (www.emmanuellutherantx.org) is up and running, and our Sunday morning worship has seen increased enthusiasm following a shift to more appealing music and messages. But we are missing you.

If you get a chance, please let me know how things are going for you in your journey. Have you moved on to another church? Did something happen here that caused you to leave? Was something within the church not reaching you? Whatever the case may be, I want you to know that I care about this and would love to find a remedy.

Maybe we can get together for coffee or lunch. Thursdays are usually best for me. Please feel free to contact me by phone, 173-555-4323 or email me at pastorjim@church.org.

Hope to hear from you soon,
Pastor Jim

ALDERSGATE
UNITED METHODIST CHURCH

23 WEST CRESCENT BOULEVARD, DENTON, OH 77443
173-555-4323 / WWW.ALDERSGATEUMCHURCH.ORG

Dear Ms. Brown,

Hope you are well. We value you and are concerned because our records show that you have been inactive for six months.

Currently, we are in process of updating our membership records. In an effort to do this housekeeping, I am enclosing a card in hopes of gathering some information from you. Please use our self-stamped postcard and send it back to us when you get a chance.

If you'd like to set up a time to talk, please call me at 173-555-4323 or send me an email at pastorjim@church.org.

Thanks so much!

Pastor Jim

Please indicate your present status:

_____Been Busy

_____Bored with Church

_____Attending Elsewhere (Would Consider Returning)

_____Attending Elsewhere (Not Interested in Returning)

_____Frustrated with Leadership

_____Issue with Other Member

_____Frustrated with Life

_____Have Transferred My Membership

_____Moved

CHRIST CHURCH

2010 RURAL HILL ROAD
STANDING STONE, MISSISSIPPI 37067
258.555.7664
WWW.CHRISTCHURCHMS.ORG

Dear Dr. McMurray,

Welcome to Christ Church. We are blessed to have you as a part of this congregation. This is now your spiritual home, and I hope you take the opportunity to find your place and make new friends.

As we discussed in the new member class, there are some exciting perks and responsibilities when you become a member here. Some of those expectations include praying for our church and world, attending worship every week you are available, participating in a small group that feeds you spiritually, being a part of a ministry that allows you to be in mission to others, and giving a proportional amount of your income. The commitment of your prayers, presence, gifts, and service will transform lives and save souls.

You now have a great number of brothers and sisters in this church who are available to you in a number of ways. There are many opportunities for fellowship and learning to become a more effective disciple of Jesus Christ. You also have a pastor who will stop at nothing to make sure you and yours are being taken care of.

Do not hesitate to let me know ways in which we can continue to minister to you.

Welcome!
Pastor Jim

Trinity Church

9005 WEST PARK AVENUE
POUGHKEEPSIE, NY 00225-5674
364-573-9473
WWW.TRINITYCHURCHNY.ORG

Dear Calvin,

I want to thank you for your recent interest in this congregation. You have many other options when it comes to choosing a church on Sunday morning, so we are honored that you have blessed us with your presence.

Maybe you'd like to take things a step further. As pastor, I am writing to ask you to consider joining us as a member. Your joining can only make this body of Christ stronger. You have abilities and gifts that God can use here to help us fulfill our vision to reach the unchurched and make new disciples of Christ.

Members are called upon to pray, attend worship, serve others, attend a class for personal nourishment, and also give financially. When you join, you will be asked to support the church with your prayers, presence, gifts, service, and witness to this church as part of God's church universal.

We ask a lot of our members. I make no apologies about it. And if that is not for you, I totally respect that and I hope you find a church that fits your needs. But . . . I have a feeling that you would like an exciting challenge and opportunity to be engaged here.

Trinity Church does not exist only for its members, but rather it exists first and foremost for the glorification of God's kingdom. The church exists so that we may be in ministry to others. I hope you'll join us on this journey, this great adventure, to love our God and our neighbor in this incredible place called Trinity Church.

Please feel free to contact me if you'd like to talk further. Call Mary, our office assistant at the church, at 364-573-9473 to set an appointment with me, or email me at pastorjames@church.org.

Very excited,
Pastor Jim

Calvary Church of Christ

ONE WINDSOR COMMONS
GREEN HILLS, KENTUCKY 54399
364-573-9473
WWW.CALVARYCHURCHOFCHRIST.ORG

Dear Sondra and Michael,

Over the last few weeks I've had the great opportunity to meet with you after the worship service. Nothing excites me more in ministry than to see God working in people's lives. If our church has played a part in ministering to you and the spiritual needs of your family, thanks be to God.

As you know, you have many options when it comes to choosing what to do with your Sunday mornings. You could stay home and watch duck hunting on TV; you could go jogging; or you could play golf. When it comes to choosing a place of worship, in our town alone you have a number of alternatives.

Would you consider taking your attendance a step farther and joining with us in God's ministry to a broken world?

Each Sunday night from 7:00-8:00 I host a coffee talk in the church parlor for prospective and new members. I would like to invite you both next Sunday, May 10. This will give you a chance to get to know some other people in the church community and find out more.

Think about it. Pray about it. And let me know if you can come. There will be childcare available if you want to bring the kids. Call me at 364-573-9473 or email me at pastorjim@church.org.

Thanks so much,
Pastor Jim

Dear Rebecca,

Thank you so much for being with our Faith Brethren Church family this week. I hope you had a meaningful worship experience today.

Our mission is to make disciples of Jesus Christ. If there is anything we can do to help you grow in faith or in any other way, please be sure to call Pastor Jim at 364-573-9473.

If you have any questions, please be sure to call me at 364-573-5792.

Sincerely,
Maria Garcia
Member, Faith Brethren Church

Dear Rebecca,

Great to have you again this morning in worship!

As we always say, our St. John's Community Church family exists to help you. So again, if there is any way we can help, please be sure to call Pastor Jim at 615-555-0033.

Please be our guest at one of our Wonderful Wednesday meals this fall. Enclosed is a ticket for a free meal to our Wonderful Wednesday dinner, which you may use anytime this fall or winter. Our meal is from 5:30 to 6:00, followed by a great set of ministries for children and small groups for adults. There are many to choose from. Please come and have dinner on us. If you need additional tickets for your family member(s), please let us know.

Just call Liz at the church office (615-444-0000) and make your reservation for which Wednesday you wish to eat.

May God's Love Grow Stronger in You Each Day,
Cherie Smith
Member, St. John's Community Church

CENTRAL BAPTIST CHURCH

201 West Main St., Henderson, Nevada 89015
(702) 555-1200 / www.centralbaptistchurchnv.org

Dear Rebecca,

It's great that you continue to worship with our Central Baptist Church family. It's nice that you feel comfortable with us.

In order for you to know more about our ministries and our Central Baptist Church family, we began sending you our church newsletter. Hopefully, you'll discover more ministry opportunities in which you may want to participate.

As always, if there is any way we can help you, please call.

May God Bless You in the Midst of All You Do this Week,
Troy Bennett
Member, Central Baptist Church

EMMANUEL LUTHERAN CHURCH

107 BUBBLING BROOK DRIVE
BREEZEVILLE CITY, TEXAS 77443
173-555-4323 / WWW.EMMANUELLUTHERANTX.ORG

Dear Rebecca,

I hope you are doing great! Great meeting you this morning, Rebecca!

Each fall, and at the time a person becomes a member of the church, we give our members a survey of the various ministries of our congregation. As a result of their completing this survey, we know in which ministries our members wish to participate and which ministries our congregation needs to provide.

Most of our regular visitors are curious about the various ministries and ask to participate in many of them. Thus, enclosed you will find a copy of this survey. Completing this survey in no way obligates you to anything, but if you complete the survey and mail it to our church secretary, Winny Baker, we'll pass the information on to the appropriate leaders. This enables us to know the ministries in which you are interested. We can then inform you of them when they occur.

If you have any questions about any of these ministries, please feel free to call me. Again, if there is anything we can do to help you, please call me at 543-6950.

May Christ's Grace and Peace Flow In through You,
Pastor Jim

Dear Rebecca,

You are definitely an active participant in worship. It is great for us that you continue to honor us with your presence. Hopefully, our Lord is blessing you through our Aldersgate UM Church family.

Would you like your own name tag? If so, please call Winny, our efficient church secretary, at 173-555-4323 and tell her how you want your name spelled.

Again, if there is anything we can do to help you, please call me at 173-674-6633.

May the Peace of God be with You,
Pastor Jim

CHRIST CHURCH

2010 RURAL HILL ROAD
STANDING STONE, MISSISSIPPI 37067
258.555.7664
WWW.CHRISTCHURCHMS.ORG

Dear Mrs. Roberto,

It was an absolute joy to have you with us this past weekend at our church retreat. I hope and pray that something in the worship experience spoke to you. And I certainly hope that you'll honor us by making a return.

I would value the opportunity to get to know you and your family. Please give me a call at 258-555-3011 or feel free to drop by the church office. Let me know if I can do anything for you at all.

Hope to see you soon.
Pastor Jim

IV. Letters Relating to Pastoral Care

Dear Emanuel,

As you know, as a minister, I am in the business of helping people reconcile themselves with God, others, and even their own personal sins and shortcomings. But I would be remiss not to recognize those times when I fall short of honoring God and my friends and family.

I made a mistake and seek your forgiveness. I have sinned against God and you, even our friends, and ask that you share with me a grace that I don't deserve.

And if there is anything I can do for you, please let me know. Can I wash your car? Mow your lawn? Do your dishes?

I'm thankful for you, and I pray this little mishap makes our friendship even stronger.

Sincerely,
Jim

Calvary Church of Christ

ONE WINDSOR COMMONS
GREEN HILLS, KENTUCKY 54399
364-573-9473
WWW.CALVARYCHURCHOFCHRIST.ORG

Dear Margaret,

Please know that I am praying for you and I pray that God is continuing to be active in your life. My prayer is also that your heart continues to mend following the loss of your grandmother.

I am always available if you'd like to talk. Please feel free to contact me.

May God Bless You and Give You Peace,
Pastor Jim
email@address.com
(C) 364-573-4231

776 WILLOWBROOK LANE, CUMBERLAND, ILLINOIS / 364-573-9473 / WWW.FAITHBRETHRENCHURCH.ORG

Dear Friend,

I am so sorry that you had a bad experience at our church. Obviously, some things were said that were out of line, and I plan to have a conversation with all the people involved to ensure that this never happens again. Please accept my apology on behalf of the church for the hurt that these people caused you. As you are keenly aware, what you are going through is painful and, while I am not making excuses, these people spoke out of their own experience.

If you'd like to talk further, please feel free to contact me. I seem to recall that you like to go to Lee's restaurant for coffee and pie. Please call me before you go next time, and it will be my treat.

You're loved here at this church, and you're loved by our great God.

Hope to talk more soon.

Pastor Jim

Dear Amber and Emil,

I am so sorry for your loss. No words can even come close to offering you comfort. Please know that you are loved and that we will do all we can to lighten your burden as time goes by.

Your church friends have already begun bringing you food and the men of the church will care for your lawn for the next few weeks, if that is okay with you. Everyone is just so anxious to do something for you, when we also know that there is nothing we can really do.

I can tell you that I am with you and this church hurts alongside of you. If questions do come up or if either of you needs to talk, please do not hesitate to call.

Your Pastor and Friend,
Jim

CENTRAL BAPTIST CHURCH

201 WEST MAIN ST., HENDERSON, NEVADA 89015
(702) 555-1200 / WWW.CENTRALBAPTISTCHURCHNV.ORG

Dear Emma,

I always have such mixed feelings when I hear about a child, actually young adult, leaving for college. I'm happy for them to try out their wings and I'm a bit sad, knowing that I won't be seeing them as often. If that's how I feel, I suspect that your feelings are even stronger.

I remember the first day I met you and Chris. We were moving into the parsonage, and he came to help. He really laughed when he brought in our snow shovel. I recall that you laughed too, until we had those six inches in January. Didn't you come over to borrow it?

A child's first step is usually toward us. Yet as they grow, they slowly begin to trust their strength and to start taking steps away from us. Our children have goals and curiosities that fuel their drive to discover new and amazing things. They do so with us ever-watchful parents cheering them on.

I know you are proud of Chris. I am too. I'll never forget that look he gave me when I introduced him at the graduate's breakfast. He was so happy. Chris's going to college marks a crossroads in his life, but perhaps also in yours. You can't be there for him all the time. But I think you have taught him well.

As much as you love Chris, God loves him more. You may not be there, but God always is. Call me if you ever need to talk.

Grace and Peace,
Pastor Jim

EMMANUEL
LUTHERAN
CHURCH

107 BUBBLING BROOK DRIVE
BREEZEVILLE CITY, TEXAS 77443
173-555-4323 / WWW.EMMANUELLUTHERANTX.ORG

Dear José,

Although we spoke at the hospital, I also wanted to send you this note. Here are some generous words spoken by the most loving person who ever lived, "Come to me, all of you who are weary and carry heavy burdens, and I will give you rest." This grand invitation of Christ is something that I turn to time and time again. I pray that these words will comfort you as well.

I am praying for Rachael daily and with your permission ask our church prayer team to pray for her speedy recovery as well.

Blessings this day, now and forever,
Pastor Jim

ALDERSGATE
UNITED METHODIST CHURCH

23 WEST CRESCENT BOULEVARD, DENTON, OH 77443
173-555-4323 / WWW.ALDERSGATEUMCHURCH.ORG

Dear Mr. and Mrs. Arrington,

I wanted to follow up with you regarding our conversation about your son. I have no intention of embarrassing you or your child, but I want you to understand the full implications of your son's behavior. While we strive to offer grace and acceptance to all persons, there are, nevertheless, boundaries that we ask persons to respect. Sadly, your son crossed one of these boundaries.

Please take a few minutes and review the code of conduct that Peter signed at the beginning of the year. As you recall, we ask our youth to sign this form, so we are all clear about what behaviors are acceptable and what behaviors are not.

I usually really enjoy being with Peter, but I just cannot put other kids at risk. I think you would agree that as the youth leader, I have a responsibility for the safety of all of the youth. So when Peter brought a bottle of alcohol and tried to spike the punch, it was more than a harmless prank. As you know, he was a little drunk and had already driven to the meeting with another kid in the car. When you and Peter talk about what happened, please let him know that we want him to come back to Youth. There is no reason why this incident has to jeopardize his relationship with the church.

I plan to email Peter to follow up as well. In the meantime I believe that you and I share a common goal here. Let me know if I can help in any way.

Yours in Christ,
Pastor Jim

ALDERSGATE
UNITED METHODIST CHURCH

23 WEST CRESCENT BOULEVARD, DENTON, OH 77443
173-555-4323 / WWW.ALDERSGATEUMCHURCH.ORG

Dear Mary and Sam,

I want you to know how much I respect the two of you. Your lives individually and communally speak volumes of your love for God, family, and one another. If there were a way that I could somehow reach into this marriage and totally remove all of its stressors and difficulties, I would do so.

Much of life is difficult, full of trespasses and faults that we must find the strength to forgive. My hope is that you are practicing that grace when needed most. But I also hope that as the two of you continue growing in your marriage, your bond becomes stronger and more vital.

Here are some suggestions; do with them as you wish.

1. Take time together to enjoy life. Go to dinner and share life! Our church offers childcare to families who want a night off. Take advantage of that!

2. Continue working on your communication. Ninety percent of all communication is miscommunication—meaning, you may think you're delivering a message, but that may not be what is received. The best book I have ever read on this subject is _____.

3. Along those same lines: If you are going to fight, fight fair. This helped my wife and me a lot. Ask me to get you the name of that book.

4. Gather with other couples. Talk about important stuff.

Then talk about unimportant stuff. We have a great new Sunday school class you might like to try.

5. Spend time studying Scripture and pray as a couple. You don't have to be scholars. Just bring the right heart and the right attitude. I've got a book of devotions that you can borrow.

6. Goof off together as much as possible. Angels can fly because they take themselves lightly.

Love you both,
Pastor Jim

CHRIST CHURCH

2010 RURAL HILL ROAD
STANDING STONE, MISSISSIPPI 37067
258.555.7664
WWW.CHRISTCHURCHMS.ORG

Dear Joel and Margaret,

How was that honeymoon? While you both were off galli-vanting together, seeing great sights and eating great food, I ate the same leftover macaroni for lunch and fought the same traffic at rush hour. But when I get home, my beautiful wife and adorable baby are there to remind me how blessed I am to have a home, and family who love and care for me.

The way you two looked at each other at your wedding says that both of you know how much the other person loves you. You'll find that this sort of love will get you through tough times like financial difficulties, crying babies, little spats, even big spats, and more.

Love each other more than you love yourself. Love God even more.

Call me after you guys get all your gifts opened up.

If you have extra stuff, I'll take a microwave!

Kidding,
Pastor Jim

Central Baptist Church

201 West Main St., Henderson, Nevada 89015
(702) 555-1200 / www.centralbaptistchurchnv.org

Dear Friend,

I want you to know just how much you have touched my life. Your presence in our church, in our community is priceless. No one can replace you. No one.

You were especially gracious to me after that bombed sermon...or two...okay, three at most. You have taught me how to be a better pastor, a better friend, a better husband, and a better father, even a better follower of Christ. You have taught me how to live without regret. And now you're teaching me something else. You are teaching me how to face the most inevitable chapter of our lives—me, the ever-impressionable student—you, the effervescent example of humility and wit and courage.

You leave us behind, but your legacy remains. I hope to honor you by passing on that same gentle humility and compassion that I see in you to every person I meet—quite the legacy, indeed.

Soon you will open your eyes and you will see the glory of God. As you do that, the light of this world will fade and the beauty of resurrection sunlight will meet you. There will be no more pain.

You know that you have a special place in my heart, but more important, you have a special place in God's.

See you soon enough.
Pastor Jim

P.S. I promise to love your family with the love you have shown me.

9005 West Park Avenue
Poughkeepsie, NY 00225-5674
364-573-9473
www.trinitychurchny.org

Dear Billy,

It was really cool that you offered that prayer request for
_____. God really loves children, and this prayer request
was something that made God smile. God will certainly be at
work in this situation. God cares about it just as much as
you do!

If you have any more prayer requests in the future, please let
me know.

Would it be okay if I asked you to pray for me sometimes?
Please pray that God will help me be the pastor he needs me
to be.

By the way, I'll pray for you too.
Pastor Jim

Calvary Church of Christ

ONE WINDSOR COMMONS
GREEN HILLS, KENTUCKY 54399
364-573-9473
WWW.CALVARYCHURCHOFCHRIST.ORG

Dear Concerned Member,

The fact that you have raised a concern with me regarding our Director of Youth Ministries says to me that you care deeply about God, this church, and our youth. I thank God for that.

I want you to know that I have met personally with Rev. Miller to talk about her ministry and ways in which it can be enhanced. We will probably also discuss it at our next Youth Council meeting. I believe the issue you pointed out can be easily fixed.

As you might know, oftentimes we have no idea that there is a problem, unless someone points it out. In that regard, we're a bit like athletes who need someone to point out where we are going wrong in our hitting or shooting. (Then again, most jobs are like that. We all need encouragement and accountability.)

Hopefully, we'll see some strides made in the next few weeks. If you are still unhappy by then, let's talk again and see if we can pursue a different approach.

Thanks for communicating about this issue. I appreciate it. Please let me know if there is anything else I can do for you.

Yours in Christ,
Pastor Jim

776 Willowbrook Lane, Cumberland, Illinois / 364-573-9473 / www.faithbrethrenchurch.org

Dear Tom,

The good news is: your little hiccup the other day will allow you to recover quite easily! The bad news is: I think this puts your quest to play quarterback for the Dallas Cowboys back a couple of years. C'est la vie, ya know! You can always tell people that your meteoric rise to the top of the football chain was cut short because of this! (Definitely had nothing to do with the fact that you can't throw a spiral to save your life.)

In all sincerity, get better. Accidents, major or minor, are never fun.

If you need someone to make a meal or come by to visit, let me know! We can arrange that.

Pastor Jim

ST. JOHN'S
COMMUNITY CHURCH

5008 ROSA PARKS BOULEVARD, NASHVILLE, TENNESSEE
615-555-9473 / WWW.STJOHNSNASHVILLE.ORG

Dear Member,

One of the most meaningful things we can do with one another is gather for a meal. In that spirit, my family would like to invite your family over for a casual dinner on Saturday, August 23, at 6:00.

My hope is we'll get to know one another better. I'd love to hear about you and your family, your jobs, your hobbies—all of that. I'll share some of my life with you too. You may be surprised to hear this, but pastors are normal people too. If you come over to watch a football game, you may even see me get a little heated.

Please let me know if you can come and if there are any dietary restrictions or preferences. Call me at 615-555-6960 or email me: pastorjim@church.org.

We're looking forward to it. Thanks so much,
Pastor Jim

CENTRAL BAPTIST CHURCH

201 WEST MAIN ST., HENDERSON, NEVADA 89015
(702) 555-1200 / WWW.CENTRALBAPTISTCHURCHNV.ORG

Dear Betty,

Thank you for all the work you are doing to make our ministry of evangelism more effective. And thank you for agreeing for offering your personal witness during the worship service next Sunday. Please speak for only 3-5 minutes; I promise that any longer than that the congregation begins to get restless.

The number one way we can attract people to a life with God and a life in the church is personal testimony. People will get excited to hear about how God is working in your life.

I also look forward to hearing you next Sunday. Please sit toward the front of the sanctuary and be prepared to come to the lectern right before the offering.

If you need any help or would like to run your talk past me, please let me know. I'm always happy to help.

May Christ Speak through You,
Pastor Jim

EMMANUEL
LUTHERAN
CHURCH

107 BUBBLING BROOK DRIVE
BREEZEVILLE CITY, TEXAS 77443
173-555-4323 / WWW.EMMANUELLUTHERANTX.ORG

Dear Mindy and David,

Congratulations on the adoption of Sammy. I know you've done a lot to pave the way for this glorious day, and I thank God that you were willing to make it happen. Your new son is uniquely blessed with the chance to call you Mom and Dad.

As a parent myself, I can promise you that there is no greater joy in life than loving and caring for a child.

May you spoil him often with love and laughter, trips to zoos, cotton candy, and so much more. May God bless you as you prepare for late-night bottle feedings, teething, and those incredibly frequent diaper changes.

Again, congratulations,
Pastor Jim

ALDERSGATE
UNITED METHODIST CHURCH

23 WEST CRESCENT BOULEVARD, DENTON, OH 77443
173-555-4323 / WWW.ALDERSGATEUMCHURCH.ORG

I recommend creating a template from which all birthday cards can be written. This way all members receive the same card. Somewhere on the card, leave space for a personalized note from you.

My notes typically read something like:

Your birthday is the one day a year that people stop to celebrate you. Enjoy it while it lasts! Tomorrow you'll be back to having to take out the trash like everyone else!

Happy Birthday!

Pastor Jim

Or

I thank God for the day you were born. Thanks for being you! Hope this birthday is the best yet!

Happy Birthday,

Pastor Jim

CHRIST CHURCH

2010 RURAL HILL ROAD
STANDING STONE, MISSISSIPPI 37067
258.555.7664
WWW.CHRISTCHURCHMS.ORG

Dear Patty,

You've done it! Congratulations! It is a little hard to believe that you've already concluded this next chapter of your life.

In this time of transition, remember who you are and remember whose you are. You are a beloved child of God and we, your church family, are very proud of you. Please accept this small gift in honor of your hard work.

If you need any career advice, call me. I know some great seminaries! (A pastor has to try, right?)

Way to Go!
Pastor Jim

9005 WEST PARK AVENUE
POUGHKEEPSIE, NY 00225-5674
364-573-9473
WWW.TRINITYCHURCHNY.ORG

Dear Joel,

Congratulations on receiving your high school diploma. Not often does life give us the chance to celebrate our own personal victories. Your high school graduation is one of those times. This has to be such a fine feeling for you!

My hope is that in another few years, I'll have an opportunity to write another letter, one that congratulates you on an equally exciting success. I believe this graduation is just another of many great milestones in your life.

As a reminder—not that a brilliant high school graduate needs one—always thank those who have helped you get where you are. Never forget those who refuse to leave you alone!

As you go forward and move on to your next adventure, remember our great God, who says, "I will never leave you nor forsake you."

Once again, congratulations!
Pastor Jim

Calvary Church of Christ

ONE WINDSOR COMMONS
GREEN HILLS KENTUCKY 54399
364-573-9473
WWW.CALVARYCHURCHOFCHRIST.ORG

Dear Scout,

There is no doubt about it, for all the hours you have diligently invested in the Boy Scouts of America, you deserve this Eagle Scout Award!

Some of the greatest men in American history were also Eagle Scouts, including Neil Armstrong, President Gerald Ford, and even Steven Spielberg. And now you join them.

Great job. We're all very proud.
Pastor Jim

FAITH BRETHREN CHURCH

776 WILLOWBROOK LANE, CUMBERLAND, ILLINOIS / 364-573-9473 / WWW.FATHBRETHRENCHURCH.ORG

Dear Mr. and Mrs. Jones,

I want to say congratulations on the birth of your first grand-child. Personally, I don't have any grandchildren—yet! But I know about how much grandparents love their grandchildren. And I know how much I loved my grandparents. For the first few years of my life, my grandmother walked to her bank every Friday at noon and deposited $10.00 in my college education fund. My grandfather taught me how to dunk doughnuts into coffee, and encouraged my interest in trains and soccer. I'm sure there will be many special times for you ahead. I apologize for my own recollections, but your recent bundle of joy just triggers so many fond memories.

My prayer is that you will find ways to share your wisdom and love with this new addition to your family.

Please send some pictures when you get a chance.

Congratulations!
Pastor Jim

ST. JOHN'S
COMMUNITY CHURCH

5008 ROSA PARKS BOULEVARD, NASHVILLE, TENNESSEE
615-555-9473 / WWW.STJOHNSNASHVILLE.ORG

Dear Friend,

Congratulations! You've done well, good and faithful
worker! Congratulations as you move into the next phase of
your life, which I hope is an exciting new route in your life
journey.

I know that such a day brings great joy, but also some am-
biguity and perhaps fear. Please know that God continues to
care for you and needs you to help further his kingdom. And I
hope that you will share the wealth of your experience in mission and ministry at our church when you are ready.

In awe,
Jim

CENTRAL BAPTIST CHURCH

201 WEST MAIN ST., HENDERSON, NEVADA 89015
(702) 555-1200 / WWW.CENTRALBAPTISTCHURCHNV.ORG

Dear Friend and Colleague,

This is just a brief note to say how much your ministry has meant to me and our church. In all honesty, I need pages and pages and entire bottles of ink to adequately express just how inspiring you have been as a minister of the gospel.

Thank you for showing me how to live and love well. If I can do only half of what you've done in the churches you have served, I'll be a very successful pastor.

Yes, you are retiring from full-time service, but, as you know, nobody ever retires from Christian service. Still too much left in the tank. Still too much work to do.

While I know you're going to be busy in retirement, I will need your wisdom at some point, I am sure. Call me if you get a spare moment!

Jim

EMMANUEL LUTHERAN CHURCH

107 BUBBLING BROOK DRIVE
BREEZEVILLE CITY, TEXAS 77443
173-555-4323 / WWW.EMMANUELLUTHERANTX.ORG

Dear Graduate,

I know you thought you'd never make it. But in reality, I never had a doubt that you would. It is clear to me that your determination to love God and your neighbor has always been the fueling passion of your life. And it is that love that got you through those difficult hermeneutical tasks, theological contours, and religious debates about traditional vs. contemporary vs. blended vs. emergent vs. ancient/future.

My hope is that you'll take the things you learned with you to use in the tasks ahead. Serving in ministry—there is no greater thing. But sometimes ministry is a bit like a desert, so make sure you are prepared and always have trusted companions at your side and make sure you have enough water—living water—in your canteen.

God is already doing great things through you. My prayer is that God will continue to equip and empower you as you expand the territory of his kingdom.

If you need anything, just call me at 173-555-0844.

Your New Colleague,
Pastor Jim

V. Letters Relating to Stewardship and Finance

ALDERSGATE
UNITED METHODIST CHURCH

23 WEST CRESCENT BOULEVARD, DENTON, OH 77443
173-555-4323 / WWW.ALDERSGATEUMCHURCH.ORG

Dear Fellow Pastors,

Here are the 10 commandments of church finance.

1. Preach on it. And we have to preach on it more than just every November.
2. Tithe your 10%. Communicate to the church what you give and why.
3. Stop communicating, "We need to give more because the budget is in trouble."
4. Communicate, "We give to invest in and change people's lives for the sake of the kingdom."
5. Know who your givers are and who your givers are not.
6. Learn what the audacious goals are of those who regularly give of their finances.
7. Instead of printing the offering in the bulletin, print a story that exemplifies a life changed by the ministry of the church.
8. Stop asking for doughnut donations on Sunday morning. Treat your people well; stop begging for money.
9. Stop treating the Sunday morning worship time as a dull drudgery. Invite lay members to testify about the power of tithing!
10. Never waste a penny of church funds. Luke 15 reminds us, even a penny is a treasure.

CHRIST CHURCH

2010 RURAL HILL ROAD
STANDING STONE, MISSISSIPPI 37067
258.555.7664
WWW.CHRISTCHURCHMS.ORG

Dear Mr. Luciano,

I want to express my heartfelt appreciation for your recent gift to the church.

And while financial gifts are confidential, I felt compelled to send a personal thank-you for your generous contribution. As you know, our church delights in bringing glory to God's kingdom and your gift will help us do even more.

Thank you for being a blessing. I hope this church and its ministry continue to bless you.

Grace and Peace,

Pastor Jim

Calvary Church of Christ

ONE WINDSOR COMMONS
GREEN HILLS, KENTUCKY 54399
364-573-9473
WWW.CALVARYCHURCHOFCHRIST.ORG

Dear Friends,

If there is one topic in the world that a congregation would rather not hear a preacher drone on and on about, it is money. And yet at the same time, financial solvency is a spiritual issue and something that churches and families so often have a hard time achieving.

No one can argue that in comparison with much of the rest of the world, Americans are richly blessed. This means that even those in what our society considers lower incomes still are on the high end of economic security when compared to the rest of the world. I share this information as a way to educate people on ways that we have been blessed, and to say that we have been blessed in ways we rarely even consider.

My hope is that you are a great steward of your gifts. My hope is that you are saving for a rainy day, saving for emergencies, saving for retirement, saving for kids and grandkids so that they can go to a college that will educate them for their chosen profession. And my hope is also that you will consider ways to give to your faith community. Stewardship is not about how much money we make; it is about what we do with what we have. That makes our giving commitment a spiritual issue. May we all be faithful stewards of the gifts God has given us.

In the next few weeks, you'll be receiving more communication regarding our upcoming campaign to help our church reach financial solvency. Please feel free to contact me or Fred Hogan, our Stewardship Chair, if you have questions or suggestions.

Humbly Yours,
Pastor Jim

Dear Friends,

A body, plant, or any living organism always finds ways to grow, but God intends us not merely to grow but to flourish. We, at Trinity Church, are striving to become the kind of people God intends us to be. In order for us to take our next steps of faith and have our ministries blossom, we need to plan and budget for the year. And whether you have been giving little or whether you have been giving much, will you accept this card and renew your commitment to serve God through this church with your financial gifts?

Please take the time to pray about this with your family. Consider even asking your children to add their insights and wisdom or to commit part of their allowance.

After you have prayerfully considered your financial gift to God, please complete the enclosed card and return it by the date noted at the bottom of the card. If you have been giving zero percent of your income, perhaps the scriptural exhortation of a ten percent tithe is too much. Perhaps you could begin with one or two percent this year, moving up next year—in order to work your way toward a full tithe. And if you have been giving seven percent, perhaps you could move to nine percent.

While you may prefer putting your check in the offering plate, the Finance Committee also recommends that you consider an Electronic Funds Transfer. Please know that we will take appropriate action to safeguard your bank account information. The designated amount will be debited from your checking account on the same day of each month. If you have questions concerning EFT, please contact Rachel Hastings, our Finance Committee chair.

After prayer and in consultation with my family, we are offering ten percent of our income after taxes. We do this because we believe in the ministries of our church and in your gifts and graces in service to this community. Since we have begun budgeting and tithing, we have found we have more than enough money to invest for our retirement and children and more than enough to live on.

Please remember that while your financial commitment is important to our church, you and your family are more important. If you don't feel blessed by God by your giving, we will refund your money. We also invite you to consider tithing your gifts of presence, time, and service as well.

Please join me in this next step of faith. If you would like to talk more about this, please let me know.

I'm always around,
Pastor Jim

P.S. "Always around" means that I'm either at the church, at home, or out participating in life-giving ministry. Chances are, I'm out! If you need to reach me quickly, here is my cell phone number: 364-573-6044.

Calvary Church of Christ

ONE WINDSOR COMMONS
GREEN HILLS, KENTUCKY 54399
364-573-9473
WWW.CALVARYCHURCHOFCHRIST.ORG

Dear Friends,

One of the frustrations I have with giving in the church is that people are so hush-hush about it. To be sure, part of that comes from Jesus' instruction to be careful about making public displays of spiritual practices that are to be done in private. There is great truth in this teaching, and we need to do our best to adhere to it. The church needs to create an atmosphere that allows giving and privacy. But much of our reluctance to talk about giving relates to our reluctance to talk about money in general and has little to do with the Bible's teaching. If we went strictly by the Bible, we would have no problem giving ten percent of our income or, as Paul suggests, offering second-mile giving.

With that said, I try to practice great transparency in this area. As the pastor of this church, I don't want the congregation guessing whether or not I follow Scripture.

Here is a breakdown of what my family gives.

I give ten percent of my income, after taxes, which is $3,000.

I also give an additional $500 per year towards the building fund.

Also, I want to be clear that money I receive from doing weddings and funerals goes back directly towards the ministry of this church.

Giving has blessed me in ways I never knew imaginable. My hope is that you too have the opportunity to give in ways that are manageable for you.

And I'll make you a guarantee. If you give to the church and at some point feel as if your money is not put toward good use, the church will refund your money. You are more important to the life of this church than your money. But as a part of this body of believers, it is in your own self-interest to let God help you break free of the stranglehold that money may have on your life.

Time to take a leap,
Pastor Jim

FAITH BRETHREN CHURCH

776 WILLOWBROOK LANE, CUMBERLAND, ILLINOIS / 364-573-9473 / WWW.FAITHBRETHRENCHURCH.ORG

Dear Church,

We are about to embark on an incredible journey of faith. In the next few weeks we have the opportunity to take our next steps of faith and claim God's promise to bless us in order to be a blessing for others. Appropriately, then, the theme for this year's stewardship program is "Blessed to be a Blessing."

Our hope is to gather $225,000 in total pledges between now and February 1.

The money raised goes directly towards our mission and ministry programs, including the building campaign, youth and children's resources, and equipment for our worship, so that we will attract fifty new members next year.

Will you join with others in this exciting time? Begin dreaming with your family about ways in which you might be involved. My prayer is that the Holy Spirit will give you a powerful testimony. If you are a witness to the grace of God acting in your life through this process, please contact me.

One thing you may want to do with your family is all sit down and count your blessings. Consider all the ways in which you have been blessed. This spiritual discipline will certainly put things into perspective. From there, begin discernment about ways in which you would like to share your blessings with others.

Blessed Beyond Measure,
Pastor Jim

Dear Member,

As we met in worship and praise yesterday, God's spirit was evident. What a great kickoff to our stewardship program. To show just how God can work in times like this, I have asked one of your brothers in Christ to share a personal testimony regarding tithes and offerings.

Greetings. Three years ago I was nothing more than a consumer Christian. I took much but gave little. Then God began speaking to me through sermons and Bible study, and soon I felt convicted about my greed. After sitting down with my wife, we both felt like God was calling us to take a leap of faith and begin giving 10% of our income.

I cannot tell you enough how much of a difference it has made. While I didn't expect anything back, within eight months of giving back to the church, I received a job promotion. One that essentially increased my salary. While this may not be the case for others who increase their tithing, it was the case for me. And I am grateful to God for this unexpected blessing. Would I have received this promotion anyway? Maybe, but I am now doubly appreciative to God. I know that God is not a vending machine; I view it as God saying to me, "You have been faithful with little—I can trust you to be faithful with much."

My life has been changed because of this church. I am committed to seeing more lives changed for the sake of the gospel.

Thanks,

Mike

Friends, I cannot add anything to this. At the conclusion of this week's service, you will be invited to come forward to the altar to submit your commitment.

Blessed to be a Blessing,

Pastor Jim

Dear Church,

What an awesome worship experience we had yesterday! I love seeing God at work. Thanks to your generosity, things are going well with the campaign. So far we have received commitments totaling _____ in pledges.

Ways in which I am hopeful God will use these funds in the coming year include:

- New kitchen for the local food pantry
- Adding a dishwasher to the kitchen to aid our monthly meals for impoverished families
- A half-court basketball pad and goal outside of our youth room
- Scholarships for youth to go to camp
- DVD players for adult education, children, and youth
- Lighting for our children's ministry room
- 4 wireless microphones, new software for our electronics team
- Funding for next year's mission projects to New Orleans and Mexico
- Also, we'll look to add a new freezer for storing food.

I get excited just reading about these additions.

Over the next few weeks, watch for people wearing small buttons with the word "Blessed." For every person who gives, we send a thank-you card with a small button. Just another fun thing we can do to raise awareness for this great campaign.

Blessed to be a Blessing,
Pastor Jim

*One Week into a Stewardship Program / **97***

CENTRAL BAPTIST CHURCH

201 WEST MAIN ST., HENDERSON, NEVADA 89015
(702) 555-1200 / WWW.CENTRALBAPTISTCHURCHNV.ORG

Dear Church,

In just a short time, we have reached a commitment by a number of families totaling _____ in pledges. Praise God.

In less than a week, we will have one more "Commitment Sunday" service. For those who have already made financial commitments, you have a chance this weekend to do a spiritual assessment of your entire life. And for those who have not, we hope that your time for a commitment is near.

This week I would like to include a note from a father who brings his family to our monthly meal.

For the first time in my life I had to take my family to the church to get a meal. I have been out of work and could not get a job to save my life. My wife has been working, but her employer keeps cutting her hours. It's just been a tough time.

When we came to the church for the meal, all that was forgotten, at least for a minute. The food was good. And our two kids were able to play with other kids in the playroom. They want to keep going back. I'm hoping things will get better so that we don't have to come back for the meal. But we do want to come and check out the church. It would be good for our family to get back to church anyway.

I am not asking you to give to a line item on a budget, I am not asking you to give so that I may improve my personal pastoral library. I am asking you to give, period. Christ is calling you, so that we might continue changing and influencing lives like the one seen above.

Praying for you this week.

This weekend, may you be a blessing,
Pastor Jim

ST. JOHN'S
COMMUNITY CHURCH

5008 ROSA PARKS BOULEVARD, NASHVILLE, TENNESSEE
615-555-9473 / WWW.STJOHNSNASHVILLE.ORG

Dear Church,

More pledges continue to come in. To those of you who have blessed this church and community, thank you so much! Please read the incredible story below. I think it will inspire you. It did me. This story is a testimony from a mother who has three children in our youth and children's ministry program. She gave me permission to share it with you.

At our old church, our kids had some friends there, whom they liked. But the quality of the youth and children's programs was sorely limited. The helpers treated the youth room like the Sistine Chapel. My kids couldn't play inside. And the yard outside had stickers and briars. Anytime they played, they came back crying.

Fast forward to your church—the helpers always have a smile on their faces. My kids learn songs, dances, Scripture, and create the nicest crafts. My kids always hate to leave. And if we have to miss Sunday morning or Wednesday night, my kids are always sad about this. Thanks so much for loving our kids and providing a safe and exciting place for them to grow in their faith. Makes my job a lot easier at home.

This is just one of the great stories I'm hearing as people tell me about what our church means to them. We all can agree that God is blessing us.

If you have a story that you'd like to share, please contact me. We are blessed to be a blessing. Help us share the good news about our church.

Sincerely,
Pastor Jim

EMMANUEL LUTHERAN CHURCH

107 BUBBLING BROOK DRIVE
BREEZEVILLE CITY, TEXAS 77443
173-555-4323 / WWW.EMMANUELLUTHERANTX.ORG

Dear Church,

As I write this letter, I am completely humbled by the way God chooses to bless his people here at our church. And I am ever encouraged by the ways in which God's people choose to respond to God's call.

We began this campaign with the phrase "Blessed to be a Blessing." Beyond a shadow of a doubt, the financial gifts and sacrifices raised through this campaign will go to bless, transform, and redeem the lives of people in need, both here and across the world.

During this special time of stewardship, I saw children offer their allowance, some even gave coins from their piggy banks. I know a single mother of two who took a second job to help raise even more money. I know a man who used to go to Starbucks twice a day. He's cut back and now has over $80 per month to invest in the church. One family I know cut back on gifts for Christmas, another family agreed to go from 200 channels on their satellite to only 100. (They joked, "How will we ever get by with only 100 channels?") This move alone will save them $10 per month.

Stories like this are rampant—stories I hope you'll share with others.

Thank you for being a blessing.

May your Thanksgiving holiday be the best yet!
Pastor Jim

CHRIST CHURCH

2010 RURAL HILL ROAD
STANDING STONE, MISSISSIPPI 37067
258.555.7664
WWW.CHRISTCHURCHMS.ORG

Dear Christian Friends,

Thank you so much for all that you do in our church and in our community. Giving to a ministry like this is an incredible example of second-mile giving.

We have made great progress in our attempt to increase our financial offering in order to do our part to usher in God's kingdom. And yet we still have a way to go.

I am including some information so that you can see where we stand and help us determine our next steps.

Currently the balance of our loan stands at _____.

The amount we are paying per month is _____.

The interest we are paying per month is _____.

If we continue to grow and increase our giving, we can mathematically save _____!

We may even be able to have the building fund paid off by _____!

How awesome would that be?

We're snowballing here. We started out slowly. But as we put more and more of our resources toward this, pretty soon we'll be rolling that snowball downhill and there will be no stopping us!

If you can help further, please indicate on the enclosed card how much you and your family believe is a possibility for you.

Waiting for the Avalanche,
Pastor Jim

ALDERSGATE
UNITED METHODIST CHURCH

23 WEST CRESCENT BOULEVARD, DENTON, OH 77443
173-555-4323 / WWW.ALDERSGATEUMCHURCH.ORG

Dear Friends,

I am particularly saddened to tell you that some of our members continue to suffer from our current economic state of affairs. While saying that, I am aware that times are difficult for everyone. These are times when it would be real easy to say, "Every person for himself."

But in reality, the gospel calls us to leave behind such selfish thoughts. Today, I am calling us all to action so that we can help a couple of families within our church. They need assistance with their mortgage, groceries, and gas for the car. And one young woman needs a dress so she can go to the prom.

Here is what I want you to do:

Prayerfully, consider how you can be of service. I will not divulge names, so this remains confidential. But I will act as a liaison between you and the family. If you are at a place to give money, please do so. Make the check out to the church; we do not distribute cash. If you would like to make a purchase and give it as a gift, that is a possibility. Just let me know. If you want to purchase gift cards, the family would welcome that too.

There are many ways to go about doing this. But choose a way that works for you.

We are all part of God's family.

Thanks very much,
Pastor Jim

CHRIST CHURCH

2010 RURAL HILL ROAD
STANDING STONE, MISSISSIPPI 37067
258.555.7664
WWW.CHRISTCHURCHMS.ORG

Dear Friend,

My hope is that the gift you receive will help you and yours in this time of need. I truly appreciate your courage in asking for help, and I recognize that it may have been difficult for you. But there are times when all of us need a favor. You never know when life is going to throw you a flat tire or some very sizable lemons.

Remember, this money is not charity. It is an investment in you and your family. While we do not expect you to repay us, we do hope that you will take the opportunity to pay it forward by helping someone else.

If you need anything else, please let me know. We have a career center and financial planning available. In addition, we have all sorts of ministries at our church meant to serve as a launchpad to help get people off the ground.

Please know that I am praying for you and your family and that you are loved by God. We offer this gift to you in the name of Christ.

May God's Peace Live in You,
Pastor Jim

Thank you for thinking of us in this time of need. Our prayer is that your financial landscape will improve quickly!

It is our understanding that this money is a loan that you promise to repay. We regard this agreement as a mutual pledge or covenant relationship with us. As part of our pledge to you, we are also offering you free financial counseling through a program at our church. We hope you take this opportunity. To find out more, please call the church at 220-789-7000.

Please fill out the information below. We will keep this record on file.

Date:

Name:

Address:

Phone:

Cell:

Loan Amount:

Due Date:

Reference:

Name:

Address:

Relationship to you:

Terms of repayment:

Signature:

Print Signature:

Counter Signatures:

Pastor:

Financial Secretary:

Date:

9005 WEST PARK AVENUE
POUGHKEEPSIE, NY 00225-5674
364-573-9473
WWW.TRINITYCHURCHNY.ORG

Dear Giver,

Thank you for your gift to the memorial fund. The church deeply appreciates it for many reasons. Your gift truly honors Mabel Goodwin and helps support our church's vision to reach more people for the sake of Christ's kingdom.

Always feel free to contact me. I know that I would value a conversation.

Until then, thanks again!
Pastor Jim

VI. Letters Relating to Administration

Calvary Church of Christ

ONE WINDSOR COMMONS
GREEN HILLS, KENTUCKY 54399
364-573-9473
WWW.CALVARYCHURCHOFCHRIST.ORG

Dear Colleague,

You and your ministry are especially remembered by this church. I hope that should you ever be in the area, you would contact me and come by for a visit. Please know that I appreciate all that you did while you were here, so if you would ever like to participate in any event or service, please let me know.

Thank you for your service in helping this congregation walk in God's path.

Your Partner in Christ,
Pastor Jim

Dear Colleague in Christ,

Before I began my pastorate at this church, I wondered, "How will I ever fill your shoes?" So I decided to write you this note. I only hope that I will be able to do justice to the way you cared for the people while you were here. They often speak of you with great fondness. While you may not have realized your impact at the time, they tell me about their respect for your leadership a great deal.

I appreciate the work you put in. It has certainly made my job easier! And just in case you begin to wonder, "Are my old friends and parishioners well cared for?" I want you to know that I work tirelessly to minister to their greatest heartfelt needs, and I strive to bring them closer to Christ. We're doing just fine, and I pray the same for you and yours.

Continued blessings on you and your ministry.

With Deep Appreciation,
Jim

Dear B. & B. Construction Company,

I want to thank your company for hearing our request and responding by submitting a bid. While we do appreciate your efforts, we have decided to go in a different direction.

I hope we can keep you in mind should we have other opportunities in the future.

Blessings,
Pastor Jim

CENTRAL BAPTIST CHURCH

201 WEST MAIN ST., HENDERSON, NEVADA 89015
(702) 555-1200 / WWW.CENTRALBAPTISTCHURCHNV.ORG

Dear Paul,

You are a valuable part of our team here at the church. I thank God for bringing you here. I thank you for all of those things that make you such a joy to be around. Thanks for being a partner in ministry, for being so gracious with those in the church, and for serving God in this capacity.

I know you've been dealing with an incredible amount of stress recently. In some regards, this is the life of ministry. Some seasons will be tough. But you're not the first to experience that difficulty. Moses? David? Jesus? Ever heard of those guys? Yeah, all of them experienced days of great frustration with their people. So you're in good company.

Pray about it. But don't waste your time worrying about this. Take what good you can from your critics. Honor their criticisms by learning and then moving forward. Invest all your energy into continually sharpening your craft.

And you'll be just fine. I have confidence in you. God has called you to be a leader, to minister in God's church. Don't let me or anyone else stop you from doing that.

Your Colleague in Christ,
Jim

EMMANUEL LUTHERAN CHURCH

107 BUBBLING BROOK DRIVE
BREEZEVILLE CITY, TEXAS 77443
173-555-4323 / WWW.EMMANUELLUTHERANTX.ORG

Dear Franko,

If your work goes the way I think it will go, there is a good chance that, as soon as next week, both of us will be too busy to sit down to read or write a letter at all.

So it is especially important for me to take a moment today and welcome you to this church.

The people here are a gracious bunch of recovering sinners. (We're all in recovery from something, ya know?) Learn from them. Get to know their stories. Pay attention to their lives. In doing that, you'll endear yourself to their hearts, much more so than if you tried to explain Deuterocanonical Theology to them.

If you have questions, please let me know. I'll check in on you and make sure you are settling in. Until then, you'll have to flag me down. Or I'll have to flag you down. I'm enclosing a list of contact information in case you need to reach anyone. I'm also sending you a church directory to help you start learning names. You'll find a package of business cards in your desk drawer.

Let's plan to get our families together soon. I'll bring my calendar with me to staff meeting and we can set a date.

We're blessed to have you. We really are. If this were a baseball draft, you would have been our top pick!

Your Colleague in Christ,
Jim

ALDERSGATE
United Methodist Church

23 West Crescent Boulevard, Denton, OH 77443
173-555-4323 / www.aldersgateumchurch.org

Dear Staff Member,

Thank you for all your work. I want you to know that what you are doing is incredibly important to the life of our church. Your gifts of time, talents, and service are making a difference in the lives of a great many people in this church and in the surrounding community.

And I'd like to offer you a reminder about the importance of your own spiritual life. Make sure you are taking time to slow down to spend time with God. You're no good to others if you're not connected to the Vine. Be selfish about this. Be 100% ruthless about your time with God.

Also, make sure you are spending time with your family. There are always going to be more things you can do at the church. As you know, church work is never done, but you don't get this time back if you miss it with your family.

Please note, I am not saying slack off on the job. When you're here, let's do everything that we can to make our ministry be fruitful and multiply. Let's work hard to bring down evil every way we can. But when you're done, go rest and go play.

You know why God took a day off during the creation, right? To prove to the world that things would not fall apart if he took a rest.

Do the same,
Pastor Jim

CHRIST CHURCH

2010 RURAL HILL ROAD
STANDING STONE, MISSISSIPPI 37067
258.555.7664
WWW.CHRISTCHURCHMS.ORG

Dear Sarah,

Thank you for agreeing to serve on the church board. I hope that you will find that this is a meaningful way to serve our Savior. Christ calls us to action and our church appreciates your call to this leadership position.

As you may recall, meetings are scheduled once every month, and the chair of the committee will contact you about meeting times.

Again, thank you for your commitment. Please let me know if I can help in any way.

Sincerely,
Pastor Jim

9005 West Park Avenue
Poughkeepsie, NY 00225-5674
364-573-9473
www.trinitychurchny.org

Dear Ted,

You are a leader in our church and have expressed an interest in helping with our children's ministry, so I am writing to you with an opportunity to serve in this important area.

I recently heard a story about a church in Missouri that, once they got serious about child care, vastly improved their community relations and church attendance. With that in mind, I am in the process of casting a churchwide vision to improve the way we care for families. I think that we all agree that we would like our toddler and nursery ministries to improve. I'm sure you have heard members of our congregation say this repeatedly. Personally, I would like to see us offer child care for more church gatherings, but to do so means finding reliable people who have a heart for children.

How would you feel about being a part of a team to help us plan to better meet the needs of our children? I'm praying you say yes. You would be an incredible asset to this dream team! Because I know you are busy, I want you to know that I don't foresee a lot of meetings. I think we can do most of this by email or by phone. I'm looking for five people to help. I don't think this can happen without you.

Please let me know.

Thanks so much,
Pastor Jim

Calvary Church of Christ

ONE WINDSOR COMMONS
GREEN HILLS, KENTUCKY 54399
364-573-9473
WWW.CALVARYCHURCHOFCHRIST.ORG

Dear Administrative Council Member,

While many of our United Methodist churches have a rocky road ahead of them, the kingdom of God is not in trouble. Read that again: *the kingdom of god is never in trouble.* So we at Calvary Church of Christ are not in trouble. But that doesn't mean that we can't do better for God.

The kingdom of God is the power of God unleashed on a fallen world. The kingdom of God is found where the Holy Spirit is alive and actively changing people's lives. I need your help and feedback. We've got to rethink the way we do this church thing. And that starts with me.

Please let me know ways that I can be a better pastor to you. I want to be the best I can be for the sake of the kingdom. So if you have suggestions, please call me and let's set up a time to have some earnest conversation. In the next four weeks, I plan to be in my office on Wednesday mornings from 7:00 A.M. to noon. I will be working on the weekly Bible study, but I've set that time aside to meet with you. If this time is not convenient, please call me and we'll arrange another time.

Your feedback is important to me. Please help our church further God's kingdom here in Kentucky.

In Earnest,
Pastor Jim

Note: For meeting times, distribute postcards in person or by mail. Use the same template for each meeting.

Name:
Committee Name:
Meeting Date:
Meeting Time:
Items for Discussion:

ST. JOHN'S COMMUNITY CHURCH

5008 ROSA PARKS BOULEVARD, NASHVILLE, TENNESSEE
615-555-9473 / WWW.STJOHNSNASHVILLE.ORG

Dear Robert,

Thank you for agreeing to serve on our hospitality team. You may very well have one of the most important jobs in this incredible church of ours. People who visit for the first time will get their first impressions of the church from you.

Please remember to:

1. Make sure that you greet guests warmly as they walk in the door
2. Be prepared to have persons available to escort guests to the appropriate Sunday school class, or wherever they need to go
3. Hand guests a brochure about our church ministries

After the service, remember to:

1. Invite each guest to return as they leave the church
2. Give each guest a personalized church souvenir
3. Make sure that each guest receives a home visit or phone call that day

When a newcomer attends three times, invite them to a coffee with the pastor. Please feel free to also attend.

If you have other suggestions to help guests feel welcome, please let me know what other ideas you have.

Thanks for Your Help,
Pastor Jim

Letter to Hospitality Team Member / **119**

CENTRAL
BAPTIST
CHURCH

201 WEST MAIN ST., HENDERSON, NEVADA 89015
(702) 555-1200 / WWW.CENTRALBAPTISTCHURCHNV.ORG

Thank you for all the work you do at our church. Without people like you, our church would not be able to serve Christ and our community in all the ways we do. God has given you the talents and gifts to help move our church forward. And I just want to take this opportunity to express my deepest appreciation.

May God continue to bless you and empower your ministry.

Grace,

Pastor Jim

EMMANUEL LUTHERAN CHURCH

107 BUBBLING BROOK DRIVE
BREEZEVILLE CITY, TEXAS 77443
173-555-4323 / WWW.EMMANUELLUTHERANTX.ORG

Dear Mi Young,

You've been a good and faithful servant. Thank you for serving on our church council. Well done! You brought great wisdom and strength to this committee, and I believe our church is the better for it.

Blessings,
Pastor Jim

ALDERSGATE
UNITED METHODIST CHURCH

23 WEST CRESCENT BOULEVARD, DENTON, OH 77443
173-555-4323 / WWW.ALDERSGATEUMCHURCH.ORG

Dear Friend,

If you are interested in serving on a committee this year, please take a few minutes and fill out this form. If you have interest in more than one area, please indicate which ones you are most passionate about. A Team Leader will contact you in the next few weeks.

Name:
Contact Information:
Address:
Phone: Home _____;
Work _____; Cell _____
Email:
Please indicate how you would like for us to contact you:
Phone _____ Email_____ Postcard_____

Interests
___Small Group Leader ___Music Ministry
___Children's Ministry ___Youth Ministry
___Young Adult Ministry ___ Nursery
___Retirement Ministry ___Celebrate Recovery
___Drama Team ___Outreach and Evangelism
___Finance Team ___ Communications Team

CHRIST CHURCH

2010 RURAL HILL ROAD
STANDING STONE MISSISSIPPI 37067
258.555.7664
WWW.CHRISTCHURCHMS.ORG

Dear Team,

Thank you for agreeing to serve on our new Networking Team. Our church board believes that this will be one of the most important committees of the church. As a church member you are called in mission and ministry, and daily you have many opportunities to interact with dozens of people. If we work together, we will be able to reach out to more people in order to make more disciples for Jesus Christ to transform this world.

In preparation for our meeting, please come prepared to share a list of referrals. The list should have the names and contact information of people you know: individuals, families, business associates, friends, neighbors who you think can benefit from being a part of our church community. During the meeting we will write personal notes, inviting these people to our church.

At the meeting, I will also distribute self-addressed, stamped envelopes with cards that will say, "I have an interest in learning about the mission and ministry of Christ Church." It will also have places for names and contact information. Please distribute these to the people you meet.

My hope is that by the end of this year, we'll have been able to increase our networking events exponentially. By the end of the year, how many people can we invite? 500? 1,000? 2,500?

Thank you so much,

Pastor Jim

VII. Letters Relating to Community Outreach

Trinity Church

9005 WEST PARK AVENUE
POUGHKEEPSIE, NY 00225-5674
364-573-9473
WWW.TRINITYCHURCHNY.ORG

Dear Ms. Jones:

Thanks for all that you do to serve our community and surrounding area.

In no way do I want to take away from the other institutions that receive assistance from you; however, I would like you to consider giving to the small and vibrant body I work with.

I am a part of an organization that feeds twenty-five families a month who otherwise would go without food. We tutor kids. We counsel battered wives and families who find themselves in financial debt. We visit the hospitalized; we spend time with the widows; and we educate children of all ages. We sponsor a Scout troop and an AA support group. These are some of the awesome tasks of Trinity Church.

My question for you this day is would you be willing to make a charitable contribution to our church so that we may continue changing people's lives for the better?

We currently have a number of families who give a certain amount per year. Would you be willing to participate in a contributing match with twenty other families?

We will put this money toward new appliances and furniture to accommodate impoverished families. Your gift will also go toward nursery resources and playground equipment.

I can think of no greater opportunity for your company than to partner with us so that you too can see lives being changed.

Let me know your thoughts and if there is any way I can be of service to you as pastor of Trinity Church. I am happy to take you to lunch to discuss this further. I will follow up with a phone call to your office this week.

Sincerely,
Rev. Jim Taylor

Calvary Church of Christ

ONE WINDSOR COMMONS
GREEN HILLS, KENTUCKY 54399
364-573-9473
WWW.CALVARYCHURCHOFCHRIST.ORG

Dear Dr. Jimenez,

Thank you for inviting me to speak at your event. The invitation was an incredible affirmation. I appreciate it more than you know. However, I'm sorry to say that I will not be available to attend. I have another commitment that day. But I believe in your cause and want to help promote it. Let me know if there is anything else I can do.

Please keep me in mind for future dates. I would be honored to play a role and help your organization.

Blessings,
Pastor Jim

Calvary Church of Christ

ONE WINDSOR COMMONS
GREEN HILLS, KENTUCKY 54399
364-573-9473
WWW.CALVARYCHURCHOFCHRIST.ORG

Dear Neighbor,

Welcome to Woodmont Parish. This is a great place to be, and I hope that you'll find this to be one of the most wonderful places you've ever lived. The schools are top-notch and the people are friendly. There is the park down the road where kids can play and climb on all sorts of new equipment; perhaps you've already spotted it. Once a year our church hosts an Easter egg hunt there.

Of course, your grocery stores are _____ and _____. There is a drugstore at _____. One of my favorite local restaurants is _____. The service is great and the food is better.

I am the pastor at City First Church. A church committed to mission and ministry, we are a growing congregation with vital worship and a wealth of programs for people of all ages. Our address is _____. Our worship service is at 11:00. Sunday school begins at 9:30. Dress is informal and guests are welcome. You can check us out at our website, www.city first@church.org.

I would like to invite you and your family to our monthly barbeque on July 18 at 6:00 p.m. here at the church. It would be a great time to get plugged in to the neighborhood. I'm enclosing a diagram with directions to the event. There is no cost.

We also host annual block parties.

If you need anything or if you need someone to feed a dog or mow a lawn while you're out of town, please let me know. We're neighbors for a reason.

Welcome again,
Pastor Jim Taylor

776 Willowbrook Lane, Cumberland, Illinois / 364-573-9473 / www.faithbrethrenchurch.org

Dear Mr. Steward,

We are absolutely honored that you have considered our facility to hold your upcoming event on Monday, February 20.

This is God's church, and we are just stewards of it. While we welcome the use of our facilities, at the same time, we must be prudent about its care. We do not charge for building use, but do require a $50 deposit to cover possible janitorial costs. The terms for use are included in the enclosed form. If you would like to give a donation, any monies received that are in excess of costs will go toward helping at-risk children and supporting their sporting and reading events.

Thank you for thinking of us to hold your event. Please contact Rudy Schooner, our church secretary, at 364-573-9473 to arrange picking up the keys, or call me at 364-573-9475 if you have questions or concerns.

Thanks very much,
Pastor Jim

ST. JOHN'S COMMUNITY CHURCH

5008 ROSA PARKS BOULEVARD, NASHVILLE, TENNESSEE
615-555-9473 / WWW.STJOHNSNASHVILLE.ORG

Dear Neighbors,

Hello! Hope you all are doing well. Your youth are invited to an end-of-the-school-year party, Friday night, June 11, starting at 6:00 P.M. and ending at 8:00 A.M. Saturday morning. This will be an all-nighter. The event will be hosted by St. John's Community Church and the youth will be staying in our Fellowship Hall. Our address is 5008 Rosa Parks Blvd. Directions to the party are enclosed as well. Youth will not be able to leave and return. Your youth are also invited to bring some friends.

We have plenty of adult supervision. At least eight adults have volunteered to help.

In addition to plenty of good food, we will play capture the flag and have a water balloon contest in the churchyard, so please dress appropriately.

There is no cost. And if you are available, we'd love for you to help chaperone. I know the other adult chaperones would love to meet you! And it will give you a great opportunity to meet some of your neighbors.

If you need more information or to let us know that your youth plan to attend, please contact William Overby, our Director of Youth Ministries at woverby@church.org or call him at 615-555-1234 or call the church at 615-555-9473.

Hope to see you soon,
Pastor Jim

VIII. Electronic Communication

Email

Email is a double-edged sword. It is fast, easy, accurate. However, there are limitations to using email in church. First of all, many people in the church do not use email.

In the church I currently serve, I began by sending a weekly email out to communicate what my plans were for the coming week, my sermon topic, and other tidbits of information that I needed to pass along. Sadly, some in the church without access to email had their feelings hurt because they were not being included. Then people wanted me to print out my emails. But then by the time they got the news, it was outdated. So then they wanted the weekly update on Sunday morning, which defeated much of my original intent of sending in the first place.

There are other problems with email as well. A good friend of mine in his first year of ministry made a huge gaffe concerning email. Messages were being exchanged between two staff members and a parent of a student in his youth group. After one particularly difficult email exchange, my friend went to send an email to his fellow staffer. The text was to read, "Wouldn't it be great if parents would butt out and just let us do what we felt called to do." You know where I'm going with this—he hit "Reply All" and just like that, a storm emerged.

Another friend of mine, out of the blue, received an email conversation taking place between a few of his pastor colleagues. Their topic of conversation happened to be the "ineffectiveness" of their colleague, my friend, as a pastor. One of the pastors accidentally sent it to my friend. My friend received it and was absolutely crushed by their comments. Email is like texting; people will be tempted to say things in email they would never say elsewhere.

The last issue to consider is emailing members of the opposite sex. You may be tempted to divulge personal information, ask personal questions, or even misinterpret comments like, "Your sermon was so good. You're the best." Be careful here. If you're thinking of sending a note that might be construed as flirtatious, don't do it. If you're thinking of sending an angry email, don't do that either.

I believe in grace, not karma. But in the electronics world, karma exists—what goes around comes around. It will come back. Now is the time to be, yes, "wise as serpents."

Facts about Facebook

Facebook is a social media website that allows users to obtain a personal profile while viewing the personal profiles of others. Within the site, you have an option to send private and public messages, post pictures of yourself and others, and post information regarding your personal preferences.

If there is a relative you've not been able to track down, there is a good chance someone they are related to is on Facebook. A long-lost childhood friend? I guarantee you, unless they live under a rock, their children are on Facebook.

Many churches have their own profile or group that members can request to join. If you join a private group, information remains private. If public, information is shared with anyone.

I recommend that every pastor develop a Facebook page. Add other adults and youth in the church as your friends. If you don't have a profile for your church, create one. Post pictures, plans, and anything else going on that might be of interest. But let's be realistic here. Remember that Facebook is part of the Internet, so it is always public. There is a risk that sending a private Facebook message to someone may be viewed by others. That is, if the recipient shares it, which gets me to some rules about Facebook.

1. Never share personal information or confessions over Facebook.

2. Never criticize a third party on Facebook.
3. Never think that Facebook is enough community for you to be satisfied.
4. Do not compliment the person; for example, "You're so amazing." Instead, compliment something they have done or completed, "Thanks for making the cookies at VBS, they were great!"

I'm not exaggerating; lives have been ruined because of on-line communication. Be careful when using it.

And at the same time, know that Facebook can be a great resource for people in your churches. Over 500 million people on the planet are on Facebook. And if you want to friend them all, you can. If you want to remind them that your birthday party is coming up, you can.

Know who your kids are friends with. Know that certain people may fabricate profiles to disguise their real identities. And know that regarding social media, this is the time to be discerning.

Texting Rules and Etiquette

Some people, including pastors, are tempted to say things in text that they would never say in real life. This has led to many instances of confusion, and sadly, even moments of sin. But when used appropriately, texting is a great resource. With teenagers it is especially useful. I recommend contacting parents of teenagers to get their permission to text with their son or daughter.

Two things to be careful of with texting:

1. Students may say things in text they would never say in person. There is a chance that if a student has been in a particularly honest text chat, they may sense a twinge of discomfort upon seeing you in person.
2. Do not let this be your primary method of communication with students.

As I mentioned earlier, texting can be very helpful in ministry. Next is an example of a text exchange between myself and a student in our church. Permission has been granted by the family to include it here.

Examples of Texting

Below is an example adapted from a real interchange with a young person from a church.

> Student: My uncles goin to war
> Me: How do you feel about that?
> Student: Idk, scared, nervous for him I guess.
> Me: He probably would appreciate hearing your concern.
> Student: No. He doesn't like knowing when we're worried.
> Me: Well, he does want to know that you care. Tell him whatever you want as long as it respects both of you.
> Student: But it will upset him. I need to be strong for him.
> Me: Tell him, "I am sad you are leaving because I care. But you are doing something brave, which makes me love you more. Be safe. Come back soon."
> Student: Yeah. That works.

Let's think about the positives and the negatives of this exchange.

- *Negative:* Impersonal, words could be misinterpreted; texting in public could be interpreted as rude. (Using a laptop in my small church setting is interpreted as "disconnected" even though I'm just trying to take notes so I don't forget.

But therein lies the issue of technology versus pencil and pad of paper.)

• *Positive:* Fast and easy. And for people who may have a difficult time expressing themselves, texting allows them a certain freedom.

Here is another texting example:

Student: I want to tell my Dad that I forgive him. I don't want him to be mad at me though. What do I do?

Pastor: It's all in the way you communicate it. Why does he need to be forgiven?

Student: He was abusive while I was growing up.

Pastor: And now you want him to know that you forgive him. You really love him don't you?

Student: Well yes. He's my dad and no matter how bad he's hurt me and this family, I can't stand to see him hurt.

Pastor: You need to tell him that.

Student: Ok. Should I say it to his face or write it down and talk about it later after he's read it and thought about it?

Pastor: Write it down. And either let him read it alone or in front of you. You could also read it to him.

Student: I think I'll leave it for him. We seem to communicate better that way because there doesn't seem to be an edge there. Can I send you what I wrote?

She ended up sending me what she wrote. It was beautiful. Later that day I received a text that said this:

Student: So my dad got the note I left him while I wasn't there and he called me and thanked me and said he loved me.

Mission accomplished. There may be a residual mark left upon this student that we'll have to address later, but for now, these texts helped God minister in such a way that an entire family may now be changed.

My attempt in these situations was to help these youth communicate thoughts and feelings they were unable to process.

Twitter

Twitter helps people make appropriate, casual, funny observations while experiencing life. Twitter invites people to experience life from your point of view. I recommend using Twitter to help you stay up-to-date with authors, politicians, musicians, mentors, and friends you respect. As you do this, you will build for yourself a cadre of friends across the country that are interested in many of the same things you are interested in.

Examples of Tweets

Here are some examples of appropriate tweets that I have left recently.

@ Annual Conference. The Bishop said something awesome, "We live in our Annual Conference." True that.

@ Home. My baby is learning to take her first steps. In time for the World Cup.

Recently a friend of mine left a Tweet regarding their support of Gay and Lesbian marriages. This led other pastors to begin responding. Pretty soon it developed into an argument. I must admit, even I misinterpreted the original tweet that precipitated the whole conversation.

One of the problems with Twitter is you are only getting sound bites of a larger story. Very easily, thoughts and statements can be taken out of context. Be aware of that as you Tweet. Choose your words, choose your tweets carefully as with all social media.